Photos

Master the use of Photoshop

In just few minutes and tips for existing users

Elli Dan

Contents

Introduction.

Photoshop was created by two brothers, John Knoll and Thomas, in 1987. In 1988, they sold the license for distribution to Adobe Systems Incorporated. On his Macintosh Plus, Thomas Knoll, a Ph.D. student at the University of Michigan, started writing software to view grayscale images with a monochrome display. This program (then known as Display) drew the attention of Thomas's brother John, an employee of Industrial Light & Magic, who suggested that Thomas transform it into an image editing program. In 1988, Thomas took a six-month school break to work on the program with his brother. The software was renamed ImagePro by Thomas, but the name had already been taken.[7]Later in that year, Thomas renamed his program Photoshop and struck a short-term deal with Barney scan which was a scanner manufacturer firm to distribute the program together with slide scanner. Using this approach, approximately 200 Photoshop copies were delivered.[8][9].

When you first open Adobe Photoshop, it's easy to get lost in the program for a moment before finally reaching for your freelancer's phone number. You're not alone in this, trust us.

It's a complex design program with much features, including a plethora of resources that can be intimidating at times. Nevertheless, Photoshop is not only for professionals.

File Format

The default file extension for Photoshop files is .PSD, which means "Photoshop Document. A PSD file is a file that keeps an image that can be used for most of Photoshop's imaging options. Layers with masks, alpha channels, text, clipping paths, duotone, spot colors, and transparency settings are just a few of the options. In comparison, many other file formats (such as. GIF or .JPG) limit content to provide standardized, predictable functionality. The maximum width and height of a PSD file are 30,000 pixels, with a2GB length limit.

PSD files are commonly used and supported to some degree by most competitive software, including Free / Open-source software like GIMP, due to Photoshop's popularity. You can export the .PSD format to and from other Adobe's software such as After Effects, Adobe Premiere Pro, and Adobe Illustrator.

Plugins

Photoshop plugins are add-on programs that expand the features of Photoshop. Adobe designs some plugins, like Adobe Camera Raw, but most plugins are developed by third parties to Adobe's specifications. Some of the programs are free, while others are paid. The majority of plugins are only compatible with Photoshop or Photoshop-compatible hosts, although a few can also be used standalone.

Export, Filter, import, color correction, range, and automation are all examples of plugins. The most common are the filter plugins (referred to as 8bf plugins), which can be found in Photoshop's Filter menu. Filter plugins can either change or generate content based on the current image. Some popular types of plugins, together with some popular companies associated with them, are listed below:

• Plugins for color correction (Alien Skin Software,[20] Nik Software,[21]On One Software,[22] Topaz Labs Software,[23] The Plugin Site,[24] etc.)

• Plugins for special effects (Auto FX Software,[25]Alien Skin Software, AV Bros.,[26]] Flaming Pear Software,[27] etc.)

• Plugins for 3D effects (Andromeda Software,[28] Strata,[29] etc.)

Adobe Camera Raw (also referred to as Camera Raw or ACR) is a free Adobe plugins that is used for reading and processing raw image files to enable Photoshop.[30]processing of the images. It can also be utilized in Adobe Bridge.

To help you get started, we've selected 12 of Photoshop's most useful resources and outlined what they do, their location, usage, and a few pointers on how to get the most out of them. Also included are some excellent tools in case you want to learn more about a specific tool.

1. The Layer Tool

I like to think of layers as sheets of glass stacked on top of one another that you'll use to create a final product. Each sheet can be modified individually without affecting the project as a whole, which can save you tons of time when making edits to individual elements of your graphic.

What does it do: A layer can be utilized for text, patterns, images, brush strokes, filters, background colors, among other things.

Layers remind me of glass sheets stacked on top of each other that you will make use of to make a finished product. Individual sheets can be edited without impacting the overall project, which can save you a lot of time when making.

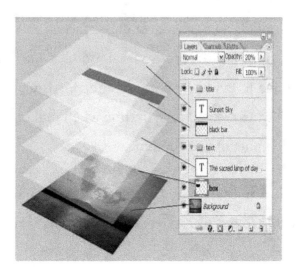

Layers are certainly the most important Photoshop aspect, and they're also, in my view, one of the reasons why so many people get frustrated. But once you figure out how they work, I guarantee they'll make your life a lot easier.

Its location is as follows: By default, it has its module in your Photoshop panel's bottom right corner. You can also get to it by going to the top menu bar and pressing "Layer."

Tip: Always give your layers a name tag. Organizing them will help you stay sane, especially if you're working on a project with a lot of layers.

To delete or add a layer:

Select Layer > New > Layer... from the top menu bar.

To choose a layer:

The layer you've chosen is outlined in blue. You must select a specific layer to edit a specific image part.

You are going to notice that each layer has an "eye" symbol next to it: click that symbol to toggle the layer's visibility while working by turning the eye off and on.

2. The Color & Swatches Tool

What It Does: The Color and Swatches tool lets you use, modify, copy, and save custom colors for your content. While this may seem like a pretty self-explanatory element, it has powerful features that will keep your visual content vibrant and unify your color schemes.

Where It's Located: It has its module on the top right-hand corner of your Photoshop screen, by default.

For Layer Duplication:

Open the Layers panel and choose a group or layer. Next, drag the group or layer to the Create a New Layer button, or right-click on the layer and select either "Duplicate Group" or "Duplicate Layer" from the context menu. Click OK after giving the group or layer a name.

Tip: Layers can be used for a variety of purposes, including, creating animated GIFs.

2. The Swatches & Color Tool

Its function: You can change, use, copy, and store custom colors for your work with the Swatches and Color app. While this looks self-explanatory, it actually has a variety of useful features that will help you keep vibrant visual content and consistent color schemes.

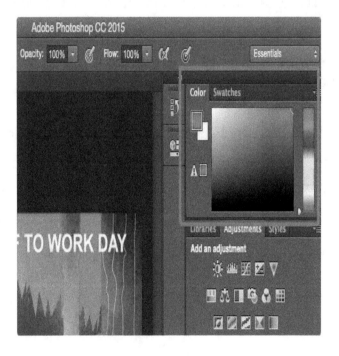

The left part, at the toolbar's bottom, is another location where you can find the Color tool. It is displayed by two boxes that are overlapping.

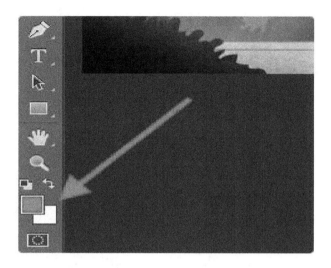

Customize your color:

Double-click the top box in the left menu or Color module to pull up the Color Picker.

After that, you will see a vertical color spectrum with a slider that you can change to make your custom color. As an alternative, if you already know the hex value of a particular color (for example, #1fb1ee), type it into the applicable box to automatically locate the color. You may also use CMYK or RGB values to choose your color swatch.

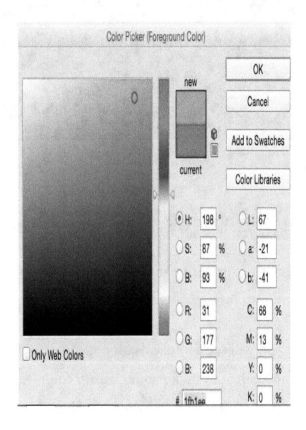

If you click on "Add To Swatches," any colors you make will be applied to your "Swatches."

Tip: Save your company colors as "Swatches" so you can refer to them and reuse them while you're making visual content.

3. Text Tool & Custom Fonts

Its Functions: The Text tool allows you to include custom fonts in your database and access advanced font settings, giving your text a professional look.

Where to Find It: At the bottom of the toolbar on your left.

All the font settings and options will be displayed at your screen's top once you click on the icon for the Text tool. You may adjust the font, font size, and character spacing, as well as the height, color, width, and style. To edit your desired text, ensure that you select the layer.

Adding text to graphic:

The text tool functions similarly to any text tool that you have previously used. Simply click the "T" icon located at the left sidebar, drag the text box over the region where you want the text to text displayed, and you're done.

Photoshop will create a layer for any text box you create. To change things up, you can change the font style, color, stroke, size, and a number of other choices.

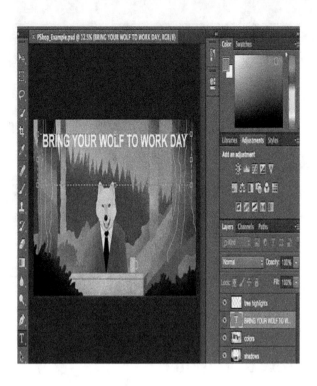

Tip: Although Photoshop contains a large number of fonts, you can still add your own.

4.Custom Brushes

Its Functions: You can include your custom royalty-free brush tips, just as you can with fonts. You can alter the size, transparency, and shape of your brush strokes using the brush settings to achieve a variety of visual effects.

Brushes are a wonderful avenue to give your content some visual interest. Photoshop offers you a nice range of brush tips that you can make use of to enhance your graphics and produce some simple visual effects.

Its location: The toolbar on the left is where you'll find it.

All the brush settings and options will appear at your screen top once you click on the Brush tool icon. These options allow you to change the brush opacity, size, and flow, among other things. There are a range of pre-installed brush tips and also custom brush tips that you installed in Photoshop.

Making use of the brush tool:

The brush tool is ideal for incorporating design elements into your work. I always recommend working with a new layer while using the brush tool so you don't intrude into any other elements. You can pick colors from your swatch library or create your own.

Changing the brush settings will glaringly alter the appearance and style of your brush. Don't be afraid to experiment a little with your personalized brushes.

5. The Select Tool

What It Is: When properly used, this tool allows you to pick individual elements, whole graphics, and monitor the items that are cut, copied and pasted to your graphic.

Its Location: The toolbar on the left is where you'll find it.

The Select tool is one of Photoshop's most basic, yet complex, tools to use. The first thing to keep in mind is that it will only work if there is a highlighted layer. So, if I want to copy or cut aLayer 4 piece, then I need to ensure that Layer 4 has been highlighted in the Layers toolbar. A flashing dotted line shows the highlighted areas.

The Select tool will be easier to use if you remember paying attention to the layer that you are utilizing.

To begin, highlight your preferred place. Then right-click and select from the pull-out menu what you want to do. You can, for example, cut objects from the current layer and replace them with your own.

Method of Selecting an image to put into your graphic:

In Photoshop, launch the image you want to make use of and use the Select Feature to decide how much you want to copy from it. Simply copy the region of the image after you've selected it.

Then open your current project's tab and paste it there as a new layer. The layer of the object(s) you want to pick should be highlighted. By highlighting multiple layers, you can move multiple objects one time.

Then right-click your pick, and you'll see some choices, such as:

A) Select "Layer via Copy" to duplicate this layer's object(s) and construct a new layer.

Tip: To select the whole graphic and layers, use the Select tool to highlight the layers. When you've found where to copy, go to the top menu bar and select "Edit" > "Copy Merged," which will copy the whole graphic and paste it as a layer.

B) To rotate, scale, flip, and shift, your choices, click "Free Transform." (If you need more assistance, see the Move tool in this post's next section.)

Pro Tip: Using "Free Transform," you can overlay PDF screenshots to create a 3D-looking picture.

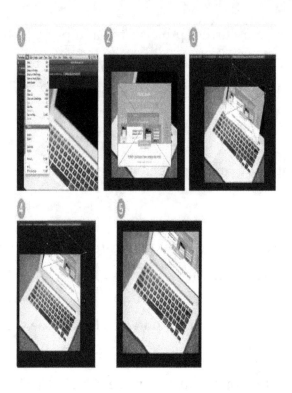

6. The Move Tool

Its Function: This is a simple tool that allows you to switch individual graphic elements around.

The Move tool works both on individual layers and theentire graphic too if all of the layers are highlighted (remember how this is done?). When repositioning text, pictures, and other elements of design, it comes in handy.

Its position: On the top side, at the left toolbar.

To Utilize the Move tool:

Simply drag the object(s) you want to move after clicking the Move icon located at the menu bar on the left-hand side.

Simply select the layer and use the Move method to move all

of the objects in it. Additional options can be accessed by right-clicking the object.

To move, rotate, scale, and flip things:

You can move, rotate, scale, and flip your selected layer's element using the Free Transform tool. To use Free Transform, press **Command** + **T** (for Macs) or **CTRL** + **T** and observe the displayed options. To keep the proportions of your elements, hold down the **SHIFT** key when transforming.

7. The Tool for Zooming

Its Function:

Its location: The Zoom tool allows you to zoom in to specific image areas while also zooming out to get a better view of what's going on.

Go to **View> Zoom In** or **View>Zoom Out** from the top menu bar to find it.

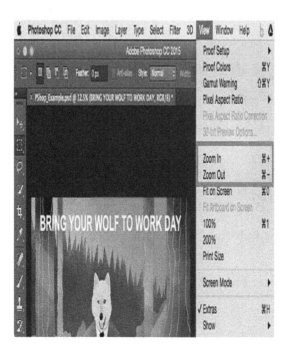

Utilizing the Zoom tool:

Also, you can go to the "View" menu and pick the zoom options (as displayed above). To zoom in and out using the keyboard shortcut, do the following; press **Command** (Mac) or **ALT** (PC) and + to zoom in, and **ALT** (PC) or **Command** (Mac)and - to zoom out.

8. The Eraser

Its Function: The Basic Eraser works similarly to the brush tool. To achieve several results, such as fades and blending, you can adjust the eraser tip's hardness and size. To help you delete unnecessary image background areas, the Background Eraser makes use of color variations.

The eraser is one of Photoshop's most valuable tools. Yeah, I understand it's just an eraser, but you've never made use of one like this before.

Its Location: The left toolbar where you'll find it.

To make use of the Basic Eraser:

If the Eraser icon is clicked, all settings will pop up at the beginning of your screen. These settings allow you to modify the eraser's hardness, size, and other aspects.

The eraser only operates on a precisely chosen layer like other tools in Photoshop. Before erasing, ensure that you have the layer you want to use.

To use the Background Eraser:

This tool is a wonder that saves time. You see how quickly background colors are eliminated from the pictures. This is particularly useful if you need an object having a transparent background.

Click and hold down the eraser icon until the menu is displayed to use the Background Eraser. Select the "Background Eraser" option.

You are now able to seriously erase. Change the Background eraser size and just press the color from the chosen layer that you want to remove. Remember to choose the layer from which you want to delete.

Tip: Don't be scared of using a big-sized eraser tip for the Background Eraser. It does not remove colors that are not being selected because it operates by eliminating those colors from the image.

9. The Crop Tool

Its Function You can crop a picture by using the Crop tool. It works similar to any crop tool you have ever used: just choose the area and crop it.

I know that is a key tool; however, you will use it as much as any other Photoshop tool particularly after your graphics have been completed and some free space at the edges has to be cleaned.

Its Location: The left toolbar

Utilizing the Crop tool:

Choose from the side menu bar, the icon shown in the screenshot, and drag the box to the region to be cropped. To modify the crop box, just click and drag the little anchor boxes that are on the crop box's corners and sides.

The canvas can be bigger than it needs to be, so you can make space for your design elements and then cut it down to the right size.

.

10. The Fill Tool

Its Function: The Fill tool, previously the Paint Bucket tool, fills a solid area with your choice of color. It is excellent for large areas to be colored or solid backgrounds. It can be used to apply image patterns. The Gradient tool in the Fill tool allows you to make a nice faded color background effect.

Its Location: Go to **Layer>New Fill Layer** in the top menu bar. The "Solid color," "Pattern", or "Gradient" can be selected from here.

Filling a solid area with a color:

First, choose the layer that you want to fill with the solid color. Then select **Layer>New Fill Layer>Solid Color** from the top menu bar. A window will appear from there, called "New Layer," with a prompt to name the layer of the new color fill. Do not worry about choosing color there, just name the layer and click "OK."

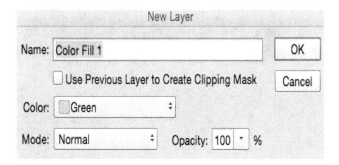

The next window to pop up is the Color Picker. You can select the solid color here that you want to fill. The color I choose at the Picker Color determines the sky color as I have chosen my background layer to fill up (this is the sky color in my graphic).

Apply Image Patterns:

You can make these patterns manually if you have patience and time, or by using a simple Google search you can find different free patterns.

Select the layer that you want to fill to add a pattern. Then select **Layer>New Fill Layer>Pattern** from the menu bar at the top. After that, a "New Layer" window will appear, prompting you to give the new color layer a name. Don't worry about choosing color there; just name the layer and click "OK."

The "Pattern Fill" window will then appear. The pattern with its scale can be selected from there. Since my background layer was chosen to fill in (i.e. the sky color in my graphic), my selected pattern of the Pattern Fill will change the sky.

Using the Gradient tool:

Next, a "Gradient Fill" window will pop up. Play around with these options, including the style, angle, and scale. To choose a different gradient than the one offered by default, click the arrow on the right-hand side of the default gradient to open the Gradient Editor, shown below:

Choose the layer that you want to fill with a pattern first to add a gradient. Then, select **Layer>New Fill**

Layer>Gradient, from the menu bar at the top. After that, a "New Layer" window will appear, prompting you to give the layer of the new color fill a name. Do not bother about making a color choice there, just name the layer and click "OK."

After that, a window will pop up with "Gradient Fill." Explore these options; the scale, angle, and style. To change the Gradient from its default, click on the default gradient's right side arrow to enter the Gradient Editor as displayed below:

11. The Eyedropper

Its Function: In Photoshop, this simple tool allows you to extract and make use of any color from any image.

It's Location: The left toolbar.

Using the Eyedropper tool:

Select the sidebar icon. Next, find the color for the extraction and click the area to clone its color.

You can see both in the left sidebar's bottom and in the Color module located at your screen's top-right once you have done the color extraction. This color box can be double-clicked for the advanced color picker, which helps you to change and store the color in a swatch for the future.

12. Options for Blending

Its Function: Blending choices include a variety of features that can be used to improve the appearance of your graphic. You may, for example, use the "Outer Glow" effect to make letters appear to glow. You can also add a shadow to the letters by using the "Drop Shadow" effect. Take the time to explore all the layer effects to see which ones appeal to you.

Its Location: From the menu bar at the top side, go to **Layer>Layer Style>Blending Options...** Also, you can double-click on a layer to display its options.

Using the Blending Options:

To begin, choose the layer to which you'd like to apply your blending effects and options. Then, from your blending choices, select the one you want to use. You can achieve a range of great effects to finish your graphics with the plethora of available options. Play around with the various layers, pictures, and texts to see what you can come up with. Here's a sample of what's available:

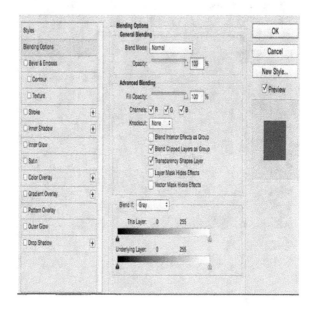

As an instance, in the picture above, I chose "Bevel & Emboss" after selecting a text layer. Isn't it pretty cool?

Before you try out your own, it's worth remembering that if you have a small budget and a tight plan, using **royalty-free stock images** will save you some money and time.

Also, for actions like modifying the canvas size, zooming in and out, making a new layer, and others, Photoshop provides a range of extremely **useful keyboard shortcuts**. For a complete list, that includes shortcuts for some of the resources listed above.

It would be unrealistic to expect you to be a Photoshop master at this point, but that isn't the point of this guide. We hope we've given you the information you'll need to use Photoshop's powerful resources in an easy, effective and timely way so that you can boost your visual content skills.

Video editing

Video editing is powerful and comprehensive in Adobe CS5 Extended version, with a simple workflow and a wide variety of video file formats like MPEG-4, AVI, and MOV formats. Video layers can be easily changed with simple key combinations, as well as other features including inserting text and making animations from single images.[42]

3D Extrusion

With Photoshop's CS5s Extended edition, you can easily transform two-dimensional artwork elements into three-dimensional ones by just clicking a button. Text extrusions, a three-dimensional library of materials, and even wrapping 2D images around three-dimensional geometry are all possibilities.

Mobile Integration

Third-party extensions have also been introduced to the most recent Photoshop editions, which has incorporated the software with a variety of applications thanks to technology like the iPad. The Adobe Eazel painting app, for example, allows users to create paintings using their fingertips and use a range of paints varying from dry to wet to achieve rich color blending. The full Photoshop engine will be released by next year for iPad, according to an announcement made in October 2018. The software would have a simplified GUI and device cloud syncing apart from the desktop version.[44]

Camera Raw

Raw files, as well as other image file formats including PNG, TIFF, and JPEG, TIFF, can be processed with the Camera Raw Plug-in without using Adobe Photoshop Lightroom. Users may use the plug-in to eliminate noise without grain adding, over-sharpening, and even perform post-crop vignetting.

3D printing tools

Users can now build and modify 3D printing designs as of version 14.1. Artists can colorize imported models, change their shape, and rotate their angles, or create new 3D models from scratch.

Tool for color replacement

The Color Replacement Tool lets users adjust the color of parts of a picture while keeping the original shadows and highlights. The Color Replacement Tool is the third option after selecting and right-clicking Brushes. The foreground color is important to remember in this tool. When using the Color Replacement tool to paint along the selected part of the picture, the foreground color will be used.

Version history

Earlier versions

From version 0.07 (codename "Bond"; double-oh-seven), via version 0.87 (codename "Seurat," which was the first retail version, marketed as "Barneyscan XP"), version 1.0 (February 1990), and version 7.0.1, Photoshop's naming scheme was first based on version numbers. Before the October 2003 release of version 8.0, which included the Creative Suite branding, Adobe released seven major and several minor versions.

Paths, Filters, Layers, Multiple effects, Revised User Interface (6.0), Magnetic Lasso and Pen, Editable Type, Adjustments, PNG support, Freeform Transform, Color Separation, Virtual Memory (1.0), CMYK color (2.0), 16-bits-per-channel support, Vector Shapes, availability on Microsoft Windows (2.5), tabbed Palettes (3.0), Layer Effects (5.0), Vector Text, Spell Check (7.0),Multiple Undo, Save For Web (5.5), Healing Brush, Camera Raw (7.0.1), Freeform Pen support are some of the notable milestone features.

CS (version 8)

As the eighth main Photoshop edition, the first Photoshop CS was released for commercial purposes in October 2003. Photoshop CS gives users more power with a redesigned file browser that enhances search versatility, sorting, and sharing features, as well as the Histogram Palette, which tracks adjustments in the picture as they are made to the text.

CS2 (version 9)

Photoshop CS2, which was released in May 2005, added new tools and functionality to its predecessor. Smart Objects, which allow scaling, and transforming of vector illustrations and images without lose to the image quality, as well as making it possible for an edit to be effected across different interfaces [50]by creating connected duplicates of the embedded graphics, were some of the most significant CS2 additions.

Adobe implemented non-destructive editing as well as the development and modification of 32-bit High Dynamic Range (HDR) pictures, which are ideal for 3D rendering and advanced compositing, in response to input from the professional media industry. A direct export feature allowed FireWire Previews to be displayed on a monitor.[50]

The Vanishing Point and Image Warping tools were implemented in Photoshop CS2.[50] By allowing users to paint, clone, and transform images while retaining visual perspective, Vanishing Point makes tiresome graphic retouching tasks much easier. Image Warping makes it simple to distort an image digitally into a form by selecting on-demand presets or dragging a control point.[50]

Camera Raw 3.0 was a new feature in CS2, and it allowed you to change settings for several raw files at once. Furthermore, processing multiple raw files to other formats such as PSD, DNG, TIFF, or JPEG, could be achieved in the background without having to launch Photoshop.[50]

Photoshop CS2 introduced a new interface that made it easier to use functionality for specific situations. Users in CS2 could also build their custom presets, which were supposed to save time and boost productivity.[50]

Adobe Photoshop CS2 (9.0) was released having an official serial number in January 2013, along with some other CS2 products, due to the shutdown of the CS2 activation servers (see Creative Suite 1 and 2)

CS3 (version 10)

Photoshop CS3 improves on previous versions' features while also introducing new ones. The simplified interface is one of the most important features, as it allows for improved speed, performance, and reliability. The Black and White Conversion, Vanishing Point Module, and Brightness and Contrast Adjustment tools have all been improved. The Clone Source palette is added, giving the clone stamp tool more choices. CS3 Extended contains all of the features found in CS3 plus a few more. 3D graphic file formats, video animation and enhancement, and robust image analysis and measurement tools with DICOM file support are all available The 3D graphic formats lets the incorporation of 3D contents into the 2D counterparts. CS3 supports video and layers formatting in video editing, allowing users to edit video per frame .[51]

In April 2007, Adobe launched CS3 and CS3 Extended in Canada and the United States. Both products support Windows Vista and Windows XP and are compatible with the Intel-based PowerPCs and Macs.[51] Photoshop CS3 is the first version of the program to run natively on Intel-based Macs.

CS4 (version 11)

Zooming and smoother panning are included in CS4, allowing for quicker image editing at high magnification. With its tab-based GUI[55], the interface is more streamlined and easier to use. With the new ray-tracing rendering engine included in Photoshop CS4, you can convert gradient maps to 3D objects, add depth to text and layers, and get print-quality output.

Adobe launched Photoshop CS4 Extended, which adds capabilities for scientific imaging, motion graphics, accurate image processing, 3D and high-end video and film to Adobe Photoshop CS4. Users can directly paint on 3D models, wrap 2D images around 3D forms, and animate 3D objects thanks to the faster 3D engine.[55]The Photoshop CS4 is the first Photoshop x64 edition for computers running Windows,[58] the Photoshop CS3 successor. The tool for color correction has also been greatly improved.[55]

On October 15, 2008, Adobe Photoshop CS4 and CS4 Extended were released. Adobe's online store and Adobe Approved Resellers were the gateways to purchase them. CS4 and CS4 Extended are available as standalone applications or as part of the Adobe Creative Suite. Both products support Windows Vista.[55]and Windows XP and are compatible with thePowerPCsand the Intel-based OS X.

On April 12, 2010,[59]Photoshop CS5 was released. The development team unveiled the latest technologies under development, including three-dimensional warping tools and brushes in a video posted on its Facebook page.

Adobe Creative Suite 5.5 (CS5.5), which included updated software versions, was launched in May 2011. Except for support for the latest subscription pricing introduced with CS5.5[61] the Photoshop version, 12.1, is similar to the concurrently announced Photoshop CS5 update, version 12.0.4.

CS5 Extended includes everything in CS5 plus features in 3D and video editing. A new materials library was added, providing more options such as Chrome, Glass, and Cork. The new Shadow Catcher tool can be used to further enhance 3D objects. For motion graphics, the tools can be applied to over more than one frame in a video sequence

Mixer Brush, Puppet Warp, Refine Edge, and Content-Aware Fill, are among the latest features in CS5. The community was also involved in the development of CS5, as 30 new tools and enhancements were requested and included. Color pickup, the Rule-of-Thirds cropping tool, Automatic image straightening, and 16-bit image saving as a JPEG are just a few of the options. The Adobe Mini Bridge is another feature that allows for efficient file management and browsing.[62]

CS5 Extended contains everything from CS5, including video and3D editing. The materials library now contains more options, such as Glass, Chrome, and Cork. You can use the latest Shadow Catcher feature to further enhance your game.

Adobe's online store, Adobe direct sales and Adobe Certified Resellers, are all used to sell CS5 and CS5 Extended. CS5 and CS5 Extended are available as separate applications or as part of Adobe Creative Suite 5. Both products are compatible with Intel-based Mac OS X, as well as Windows 7, Windows Vista, and Windows XP.

CS6 (version 13)

Photoshop CS6, which was released in May 2012, included new design tools as well as a redesigned interface[64] that prioritized performance. The Content-Aware tool now includes new features like Content-Aware Move and Content-Aware Patch.[65]

Adobe Photoshop CS6 introduced a video editing tool suite. Exposure, color modifications, and also layers, are only a few of the features included in this latest edition. After finishing editing, the user is given several options for exporting to a variety of common formats.[66]

In Photoshop CS6, there is the "straighten' tool of which a user can draw a line on any part of an image and the canvas will readjust the drawn line to a horizontal position, thereby adjusting the media accordingly. This was made with the purpose of users drawing a line that is parallel to a plane on the image and reorienting the image given that plane to achieve those viewpoints more easily.[66]

Background saving is possible in CS6, which means that you can edit an image while another document is self-archiving and compiling. CS6 also has a customizable auto-save function that ensures that no job is lost.[66]

Adobe discontinued support for Windows XP (including Windows XP Professional x64 Edition) with version 13.1.3; the most recent version that operates on Windows XP is 13.0.1. Adobe also revealed that, in favor of the latest Creative Cloud subscriptions, CS6 will be the last suite that will be sold with permanent licenses, though they will still provide bug fixes, OS compatibility support, and security updates as required.[67]

After January 9, 2017, CS6 will no longer be available to buy, leaving only Creative Cloud licenses as the purchase option remaining.[68]

CC (version 14)

On June 18, 2013, Adobe Photoshop CC (14.0) was released. It has only be made available as a part of a Creative Cloud subscription as the next big edition after CS6. Intelligent Up sampling, New Smart Sharpen, and Camera Shake Reduction for minimizing blur caused by camera shake are among this version's main features. Also included were editable rounded rectangles as well as an upgrade to Adobe Camera Raw (8.0).[69]

Adobe has launched two more feature-rich updates since the initial launch. Version 14.1, the first, was released on September 9, 2013. Adobe Generator, a Node. is-based framework for building Photoshop plug-ins, was one of the most notable additions in this version. Photoshop 14.1 came pre-installed with two plug-ins: one was to generate image objects that are based on the layer name's extension while the other was to automatically generate Adobe Edge Reflow assets.

On January 15, 2014, version 14.2 was launched with main features such as Linked Smart Objects, Perspective Warp, and 3D Printing support.

CC 2014 (version 15)

On June 18, 2014, Adobe Photoshop CC 2014 (15.0) was announced. Content-aware tools have been improved, two new blur tools (path and spin blur) have been added, and a new focus mask function has been added that allows the user to pick sections of an image depending on if they are in focus or not. Other small enhancements have been made, such as speed changes for specific tasks[72][73]

CC 2015 (version 16 and version 17)

On June 15, 2015, Adobe Photoshop CC 2015 was announced. Adobe also introduced several new creative tools, such as Adobe Stock, a library of custom stock images. It also allows for multiple layer types. It gives Photoshop a cleaner and more reliable appearance.

CC 2017 (version 18)

On November 2, 2016, Adobe Photoshop CC 2017 was announced. It added a new template selector when making new documents, as well as the ability to search for Photoshop panels, tools, and articles for help, as well as SVG OpenType fonts support and other minor enhancements. A minor update was released in December 2016 that added support for the MacBook Pro Touch Bar.

CC 2018 (version 19)

On October 18, 2017, Adobe Photoshop CC 2018 (version 19) was released. Brush organization was overhauled, giving room for more properties (such as opacity and color) to be saved for each brush and also for brush organization to be done into folders and sub-folders.

Variable font support, copy-paste layers, select subject, enhanced tooltips, PNG compression, 360 panoramas and HEIF support, symmetry mode, increased maximum zoom level, algorithm enhancements to selection tools and Face-aware, improved image resizing, color and luminance range masking, and file opening performance improvements, brush strokes, and filters, are just a few of the new features.[78]

CC 2019 (version 20)

On October 15, 2018, Adobe Photoshop CC 2019 was announced. The 32-bit Windows version is no longer supported in Photoshop CC 2019 (version 20.0). This version added the Frame Tool, a new tool for creating image placeholder frames.Proportionally transform without making use of the Shift key, distribute spacing the same way it is done in Illustrator, see longer layer names, fit font with Japanese fonts, scale UI to font, flip document view, reference point that is hidden by default, new compositing engine that provides a better compositing architecture that is easier to optimize on all platforms, a new compositing engine that provides a more modern compositing architecture that is compatible with all platform optimization.

2020 (version 21)

On November 4, 2019, Adobe Photoshop 2020 was announced. Many new and improved features are included in Version 21, including a new tool for object selection which is for automating complex selections, a new properties screen, improved transform warp, new keyboard shortcuts for brush and paint, and the option for background image removal. It improved the current content-aware fill and the tab for new documents. Also included are better lens blur, a one-click layer content zoom, and the support for animated GIF.

Photoshop can now iteratively fill several imageareas without having to exit the content-aware fill workspace in the February 2020 update (version 21.1). This version enhanced the GPU-based quality of the GPU-based lens blur and provided performance enhancements like smoother panning, and document zooming and navigation to speed up your workflow.

Photoshop Mix

Photoshop Mix is a touchscreen and tablet device-specific substitute for Photoshop Touch. Many of the features found in the desktop version are included, such as layers, filters, adjustment, and selection tools. Adobe Creative Cloud may be used to sync edited files. Photoshop Mix is an Android and iOS app. Photoshop Sketch (a simple drawing tool) and Photoshop Fix (a Photo Correction app) are its two siblings.